OEDIPUS KING OF THEBES

BY

SOPHOCLES

TRANSLATED INTO ENGLISH RHYMING VERSE WITH EXPLANATORY NOTES

BY

GILBERT MURRAY

Happy Hour Books

Published by:
HAPPY HOUR BOOKS
www.happyhoursbooks.com
email: happyhourbooks1@gmail.com

First published by Happy Hour Books 2024

Title : **Oedipus Rex**
Paperback ISBN : 9789358481495
Hardback ISBN : 9789358483376

PREFACE

If I have turned aside from Euripides for a moment and attempted a translation of the great stage masterpiece of Sophocles, my excuse must be the fascination of this play, which has thrown its spell on me as on many other translators. Yet I may plead also that as a rule every diligent student of these great works can add something to the discoveries of his predecessors, and I think I have been able to bring out a few new points in the old and much-studied *Oedipus*, chiefly points connected with the dramatic technique and the religious atmosphere.

Mythologists tell us that Oedipus was originally a daemon haunting Mount Kithairon, and Jocasta a form of that Earth-Mother who, as Aeschylus puts it, "bringeth all things to being, and when she hath reared them receiveth again their seed into her body" (*Choephori*, 127: cf. Crusius, *Beiträge z. Gr. Myth*, 21). That stage of the story lies very far behind the consciousness of Sophocles. But there does cling about both his hero and his heroine a great deal of very primitive atmosphere. There are traces in Oedipus of the pre-hellenic Medicine King, the *Basileus* who is also a *Theos*, and can make rain or blue sky, pestilence or fertility. This explains many things in the Priest's first speech, in the attitude of the Chorus, and in Oedipus' own language after [Pg vi]the discovery. It partly explains the hostility of Apollo, who is not a mere motiveless Destroyer but a true Olympian crushing his Earth-born rival. And in the same way the peculiar royalty of Jocasta, which makes Oedipus at times seem not the King but the Consort of the Queen, brings her near to that class of consecrated queens described in Dr. Frazer's *Lectures on the Kingship*, who are "honoured as no woman now living on the earth."

The story itself, and the whole spirit in which Sophocles has treated it, belong not to the fifth century but to that terrible and romantic past from which the fifth century poets usually drew their material. The atmosphere of brooding dread, the pollution, the curses; the "insane and beastlike cruelty," as an ancient Greek commentator calls it, of piercing the exposed child's feet in order to ensure its death and yet avoid having actually murdered it (*Schol. Eur. Phoen.*, 26); the whole treatment of the parricide and incest, not as moral offences capable of being rationally judged or even excused as unintentional, but as monstrous and inhuman pollutions, the last limit of imaginable horror: all these things take us back to dark regions of pre-classical and even pre-homeric belief. We have no right to suppose that Sophocles thought of the involuntary parricide and metrogamy as the people in his play do. Indeed, considering the general tone of his contemporaries and friends, we may safely assume that he did not. But at any rate he has allowed no breath of later enlightenment to disturb the primaeval gloom of his atmosphere.

Does this in any way make the tragedy insincere? [Pg vii]I think not. We know that people did feel and think about "pollution" in the way which Sophocles represents; and if they so felt, then the tragedy was there.

I think these considerations explain the remarkable absence from this play of any criticism of life or any definite moral judgment. I know that some commentators have found in it a "humble and unquestioning piety," but I cannot help suspecting that what they saw was only a reflection from their own pious and unquestioning minds. Man is indeed shown as a "plaything of Gods," but of Gods strangely and incomprehensibly malignant, whose ways there is no attempt to explain or justify. The original story, indeed, may have had one of its roots in a Theban "moral tale." Aelian (*Varia Historia*, 2, 7) tells us that the exposure of a child was forbidden by Theban Law. The state of feeling which produced this law, against the immensely strong conception of the *patria potestas*, may also have produced a folklore story telling how a boy once was exposed, in a peculiarly cruel way, by his wicked parents, and how Heaven preserved him to take upon both of them a vengeance which showed that the unnatural father had no longer a father's sanctity nor the unnatural mother a mother's. But, as far as Sophocles is concerned, if anything in the nature of a criticism of life has been admitted into the play at all, it seems to be only a flash or two of that profound and pessimistic arraignment of the ruling powers which in other plays also opens at times like a sudden abyss across the smooth surface of his art.

[Pg viii]There is not much philosophy in the *Oedipus*. There is not, in comparison with other Greek plays, much pure poetry. What there is, is drama; drama of amazing grandeur and power. In respect of plot no Greek play comes near it. It contains no doubt a few points of unsophisticated technique such as can be found in all ancient and nearly all modern drama; for instance, the supposition that Oedipus has never inquired into the death of his predecessor on the throne. But such flaws are external, not essential. On the whole, I can only say that the work of translation has made me feel even more strongly than before the extraordinary grip and reality of the dialogue, the deftness of the construction, and, except perhaps for a slight drop in the Creon scene, the unbroken crescendo of tragedy from the opening to the close.

Where plot-interest is as strong as it is in the *Oedipus*, character-interest is apt to be comparatively weak. Yet in this play every character is interesting, vital, and distinct. Oedipus himself is selected by Aristotle as the most effective kind of tragic hero, because, first, he has been great and glorious, and secondly he has not been "pre-eminently virtuous or just." This is true in its way. Oedipus is too passionate to be just; but he is at least noble in his impetuosity, his devotion, and his absolute truthfulness. It is important to realise that at the beginning of the play he is prepared for an oracle commanding him to die for his people (pp. 6, 7). And he never thinks of refusing that "task" any more than he tries to elude the doom that actually comes, or to conceal [Pg ix]any fact that tells against him. If Oedipus had been an ordinary man the play would have been a very different and a much poorer thing.

Jocasta is a wonderful study. Euripides might have brought her character out more explicitly and more at length, but even he could not have made her more living or more tragic, or represented more subtly in her relation to Oedipus both the mother's protecting love and the mother's authority. As for her "impiety," of which the old commentaries used to speak with much disapproval, the essential fact in her life is that both her innocence and her happiness have, as she believes, been poisoned by the craft of priests. She and Laïus both "believed a bad oracle": her terror and her love for her husband made her consent to an infamous act of cruelty to her own child, an act of which the thought sickens her still, and about which she cannot, when she tries, speak the whole truth. (See note on p. 42.) And after all her crime was for nothing! The oracle proved to be a lie. Never again will she believe a priest.

As to Tiresias, I wish to ask forgiveness for an unintelligent criticism made twelve years ago in my *Ancient Greek Literature*, p. 240. I assumed then, what I fancy was a common assumption, that Tiresias was a "sympathetic" prophet, compact of wisdom and sanctity and all the qualities which beseem that calling; and I complained that he did not consistently act as such. I was quite wrong. Tiresias is not anything so insipid. He is a study of a real type, and a type which all the tragedians knew. The character of the professional seer or "man of God" has in the imagination of most ages fluctuated between two [Pg x]poles. At one extreme are sanctity and superhuman wisdom; at the other fraud and mental disease, self-worship aping humility and personal malignity in the guise of obedience to God. There is a touch of all these qualities, good and bad alike, in Tiresias. He seems to me a most life-like as well as a most dramatic figure.

As to the Chorus, it generally plays a smaller part in Sophocles than in Euripides and Aeschylus, and the *Oedipus* forms no exception to that rule. It seems to me that Sophocles was feeling his way towards a technique which would have approached that of the New Comedy or even the Elizabethan stage, and would perhaps have done without a Chorus altogether. In Aeschylus Greek tragedy had been a thing of traditional forms and clear-cut divisions; the religious ritual showed through, and the visible gods and the disguised dancers were allowed their full value. And Euripides in the matter of outward formalism went back to the Aeschylean type and even beyond it: prologue, chorus, messenger, visible god, all the traditional forms were left clear-cut and undisguised and all developed to full effectiveness on separate and specific lines. But Sophocles worked by blurring his structural outlines just as he blurs the ends of his verses. In him the traditional divisions are all made less distinct, all worked over in the direction of greater naturalness, at any rate in externals. This was a very great gain, but of course some price had to be paid for it. Part of the price was that Sophocles could never attempt the tremendous choric effects which Euripides achieves in such plays as the *Bacchae* and the *Trojan Women*. His lyrics, great as they [Pg xi]sometimes are, move their wings less boldly. They seem somehow tied to their particular place in the tragedy, and they have not quite the strength to lift the whole drama bodily aloft with them.... At least that is my feeling. But I realise that this may be only the complaint of an unskilful translator, blaming his material for his own defects of vision.

In general, both in lyrics and in dialogue, I believe I have allowed myself rather less freedom than in translating Euripides. This is partly because the writing of Euripides, being less business-like and more penetrated by philosophic reflections and by subtleties of technique, actually needs more thorough re-casting to express it at all adequately; partly because there is in Sophocles, amid all his passion and all his naturalness, a certain severe and classic reticence, which, though impossible really to reproduce by any method, is less misrepresented by occasional insufficiency than by habitual redundance.

I have asked pardon for an ill deed done twelve years ago. I should like to end by speaking of a benefit older still, and express something of the gratitude I feel to my old master, Francis Storr, whose teaching is still vivid in my mind and who first opened my eyes to the grandeur of the *Oedipus*.

G. M.

CHARACTERS IN THE PLAY

OEDIPUS, *supposed son of Polybus, King of Corinth; now elected King of Thebes.*

JOCASTA, *Queen of Thebes; widow of Laïus, the late King, and now wife to Oedipus.*

CREON, *a Prince of Thebes, brother to Jocasta.*

TIRESIAS, *an old blind seer.*

PRIEST OF ZEUS.

A STRANGER *from Corinth.*

A SHEPHERD *of King Laïus.*

A MESSENGER *from the Palace.*

CHORUS of the Elders of Thebes.

A Crowd of Suppliants, men, women, and children.

The following do not appear in the play but are frequently mentioned:—

LAÏUS *(pronounced as three syllables, Lá-i-us), the last King of Thebes before Oedipus.*

CADMUS, *the founder of Thebes; son of Agênor, King of Sidon.*

POLYBUS AND MEROPÊ, *King and Queen of Corinth, supposed to be the father and mother of Oedipus.*

APOLLO, *the God specially presiding over the oracle of Delphi and the island Delos: he is also called* PHOEBUS, *the pure;* LOXIAS, *supposed to mean "He of the Crooked Words"; and* LYKEIOS, *supposed to mean "Wolf-God." He is also the great Averter of Evil, and has names from the cries "I-ê" (pronounced "Ee-ay") and "Paian," cries for healing or for the frightening away of evil influences.*

KITHAIRON, *a mass of wild mountain south-west of Thebes.*

ARGUMENT

While Thebes was under the rule of LAÏUS and JOCASTA there appeared a strange and monstrous creature, "the riddling Sphinx," "the She-Wolf of the woven song," who in some unexplained way sang riddles of death and slew the people of Thebes. LAÏUS went to ask aid of the oracle of Delphi, but was slain mysteriously on the road. Soon afterwards there came to Thebes a young Prince of Corinth, OEDIPUS, who had left his home and was wandering. He faced the Sphinx and read her riddle, whereupon she flung herself from her rock and died. The throne being vacant was offered to OEDIPUS, and with it the hand of the Queen, JOCASTA.

Some ten or twelve years afterwards a pestilence has fallen on Thebes. At this point the play begins.

The date of the first production of the play is not known, but was probably about the year 425 B.C.

OEDIPUS, KING OF THEBES

SCENE.—*Before the Palace of* OEDIPUS *at Thebes. A crowd of suppliants of all ages are waiting by the altar in front and on the steps of the Palace; among them the* PRIEST OF ZEUS. *As the Palace door opens and* OEDIPUS *comes out all the suppliants with a cry move towards him in attitudes of prayer, holding out their olive branches, and then become still again as he speaks.*

OEDIPUS

My children, fruit of Cadmus' ancient tree

New springing, wherefore thus with bended knee

Press ye upon us, laden all with wreaths

And suppliant branches? And the city breathes

Heavy with incense, heavy with dim prayer

And shrieks to affright the Slayer.—Children, care

For this so moves me, I have scorned withal

Message or writing: seeing 'tis I ye call,

'Tis I am come, world-honoured Oedipus.

Old Man, do thou declare—the rest have thus

Their champion—in what mood stand ye so still,

In dread or sure hope? Know ye not, my will

Is yours for aid 'gainst all? Stern were indeed

The heart that felt not for so dire a need.

PRIEST.

O Oedipus, who holdest in thy hand

My city, thou canst see what ages stand
At these thine altars; some whose little wing
Scarce flieth yet, and some with long living
O'erburdened; priests, as I of Zeus am priest,
And chosen youths: and wailing hath not ceased
Of thousands in the market-place, and by
Athena's two-fold temples and the dry
Ash of Ismênus' portent-breathing shore.
For all our ship, thou see'st, is weak and sore
Shaken with storms, and no more lighteneth
Her head above the waves whose trough is death.
She wasteth in the fruitless buds of earth,
In parchèd herds and travail without birth
Of dying women: yea, and midst of it
A burning and a loathly god hath lit
Sudden, and sweeps our land, this Plague of power;
Till Cadmus' house grows empty, hour by hour,
And Hell's house rich with steam of tears and blood.
O King, not God indeed nor peer to God
We deem thee, that we kneel before thine hearth,
Children and old men, praying; but of earth
A thing consummate by thy star confessed
Thou walkest and by converse with the blest;
Who came to Thebes so swift, and swept away

The Sphinx's song, the tribute of dismay,
That all were bowed beneath, and made us free.
A stranger, thou, naught knowing more than we,
Nor taught of any man, but by God's breath
Filled, thou didst raise our life. So the world saith;
So we say.
Therefore now, O Lord and Chief,
We come to thee again; we lay our grief
On thy head, if thou find us not some aid.
Perchance thou hast heard Gods talking in the shade
Of night, or eke some man: to him that knows,
Men say, each chance that falls, each wind that blows
Hath life, when he seeks counsel. Up, O chief
Of men, and lift thy city from its grief;
Face thine own peril! All our land doth hold
Thee still our saviour, for that help of old:
Shall they that tell of thee hereafter tell
"By him was Thebes raised up, and after fell!"
Nay, lift us till we slip no more. Oh, let
That bird of old that made us fortunate
Wing back; be thou our Oedipus again.
And let thy kingdom be a land of men,
Not emptiness. Walls, towers, and ships, they all
Are nothing with no men to keep the wall.

OEDIPUS.

My poor, poor children! Surely long ago
I have read your trouble. Stricken, well I know,
Ye all are, stricken sore: yet verily
Not one so stricken to the heart as I.
Your grief, it cometh to each man apart
For his own loss, none other's; but this heart
For thee and me and all of us doth weep.
Wherefore it is not to one sunk in sleep
Ye come with waking. Many tears these days
For your sake I have wept, and many ways
Have wandered on the beating wings of thought.
And, finding but one hope, that I have sought
And followed. I have sent Menoikeus' son,
Creon, my own wife's brother, forth alone
To Apollo's House in Delphi, there to ask
What word, what deed of mine, what bitter task,
May save my city.

And the lapse of days
Reckoned, I can but marvel what delays
His journey. 'Tis beyond all thought that thus
He comes not, beyond need. But when he does,
Then call me false and traitor, if I flee
Back from whatever task God sheweth me.

PRIEST.

At point of time thou speakest. Mark the cheer
Yonder. Is that not Creon drawing near?

[They all crowd to gaze where **CREON** *is approaching in the distance.*

OEDIPUS.

O Lord Apollo, help! And be the star
That guides him joyous as his seemings are!

PRIEST.

Oh! surely joyous! How else should he bear
That fruited laurel wreathed about his hair?

OEDIPUS.

We soon shall know.—'Tis not too far for one
Clear-voiced.
(Shouting) Ho, brother! Prince! Menoikeus' son,
What message from the God?

CREON (from a distance).

Message of joy!

Enter **CREON**

I tell thee, what is now our worst annoy,
If the right deed be done, shall turn to good.

[The crowd, which has been full of excited hope, falls to doubt and disappointment.

OEDIPUS.

Nay, but what is the message? For my blood
Runs neither hot nor cold for words like those.

CREON.

Shall I speak now, with all these pressing close,
Or pass within?—To me both ways are fair.

OEDIPUS.

Speak forth to all! The grief that these men bear
Is more than any fear for mine own death.

CREON.

I speak then what I heard from God.—Thus saith
Phoebus, our Lord and Seer, in clear command.
An unclean thing there is, hid in our land,
Eating the soil thereof: this ye shall cast
Out, and not foster till all help be past.

OEDIPUS.

How cast it out? What was the evil deed?

CREON.

Hunt the men out from Thebes, or make them bleed
Who slew. For blood it is that stirs to-day.

OEDIPUS.

Who was the man they killed? Doth Phoebus say?

CREON.

O King, there was of old King Laïus
In Thebes, ere thou didst come to pilot us.

OEDIPUS.

I know: not that I ever saw his face.

CREON.

'Twas he. And Loxias now bids us trace
And smite the unknown workers of his fall.

OEDIPUS.

Where in God's earth are they? Or how withal
Find the blurred trail of such an ancient stain?

CREON.

In Thebes, he said.—That which men seek amain
They find. 'Tis things forgotten that go by.

OEDIPUS.

And where did Laïus meet them? Did he die
In Thebes, or in the hills, or some far land?

CREON.

To ask God's will in Delphi he had planned
His journey. Started and returned no more.

OEDIPUS.

And came there nothing back? No message, nor

None of his company, that ye might hear?

CREON.

They all were slain, save one man; blind with fear

He came, remembering naught—or almost naught.

OEDIPUS.

And what was that? One thing has often brought

Others, could we but catch one little clue.

CREON.

'Twas not one man, 'twas robbers—that he knew—

Who barred the road and slew him: a great band.

OEDIPUS.

Robbers?... What robber, save the work was planned

By treason here, would dare a risk so plain?

CREON.

So some men thought. But Laïus lay slain,

And none to avenge him in his evil day.

OEDIPUS.

And what strange mischief, when your master lay

Thus fallen, held you back from search and deed?

CREON.

The dark-songed Sphinx was here. We had no heed

Of distant sorrows, having death so near.

OEDIPUS.

It falls on me then. I will search and clear
This darkness.—Well hath Phoebus done, and thou
Too, to recall that dead king, even now,
And with you for the right I also stand,
To obey the God and succour this dear land.
Nor is it as for one that touches me
Far off; 'tis for mine own sake I must see
This sin cast out. Whoe'er it was that slew
Laïus, the same wild hand may seek me too:
And caring thus for Laïus, is but care
For mine own blood.—Up! Leave this altar-stair,
Children. Take from it every suppliant bough.
Then call the folk of Thebes. Say, 'tis my vow
To uphold them to the end. So God shall crown
Our greatness, or for ever cast us down.

[He goes in to the Palace.

PRIEST.

My children, rise.—The King most lovingly
Hath promised all we came for. And may He
Who sent this answer, Phoebus, come confessed
Helper to Thebes, and strong to stay the pest.

[The suppliants gather up their boughs and stand at the side. The chorus of Theban elders enter.

CHORUS.

[They speak of the Oracle which they have not yet heard, and cry to Apollo by his special cry "I-ê."

A Voice, a Voice, that is borne on the Holy Way!
What art thou, O Heavenly One, O Word of the Houses of Gold?
Thebes is bright with thee, and my heart it leapeth; yet is it cold,
And my spirit faints as I pray.
I-ê! I-ê!
What task, O Affrighter of Evil, what task shall thy people essay?
One new as our new-come affliction,
Or an old toil returned with the years?
Unveil thee, thou dread benediction,
Hope's daughter and Fear's.

[They pray to Athena, Artemis, and Apollo.

Zeus-Child that knowest not death, to thee I pray,
O Pallas; next to thy Sister, who calleth Thebes her own,
Artemis, named of Fair Voices, who sitteth her orbèd throne
In the throng of the market way:
And I-ê! I-ê!
Apollo, the Pure, the Far-smiter; O Three that keep evil away,
If of old for our city's desire,
When the death-cloud hung close to her brow,
Ye have banished the wound and the fire,
Oh! come to us now!

[They tell of the Pestilence.

Wounds beyond telling; my people sick unto death;
And where is the counsellor, where is the sword of thought?
And Holy Earth in her increase perisheth:
The child dies and the mother awaketh not.

I-ê! I-ê!

We have seen them, one on another, gone as a bird is gone,
Souls that are flame; yea, higher,
Swifter they pass than fire,
To the rocks of the dying Sun.

[They end by a prayer to Athena,

Their city wasteth unnumbered; their children lie
Where death hath cast them, unpitied, unwept upon.
The altars stand, as in seas of storm a high
Rock standeth, and wives and mothers grey thereon
Weep, weep and pray.
Lo, joy-cries to fright the Destroyer; a flash in the dark they rise,
Then die by the sobs overladen.
Send help, O heaven-born Maiden,
Let us look on the light of her eyes!

[To Zeus, that he drive out the Slayer,

And Ares, the abhorred
Slayer, who bears no sword,
But shrieking, wrapped in fire, stands over me,

Make that he turn, yea, fly
Broken, wind-wasted, high
Down the vexed hollow of the Vaster Sea;
Or back to his own Thrace,
To harbour shelterless.
Where Night hath spared, he bringeth end by day.
Him, Him, O thou whose hand
Beareth the lightning brand,
O Father Zeus, now with thy thunder, slay and slay!

[To Apollo, Artemis, and Dionysus.

Where is thy gold-strung bow,
O Wolf-god, where the flow
Of living shafts unconquered, from all ills
Our helpers? Where the white
Spears of thy Sister's light,
Far-flashing as she walks the wolf-wild hills?
And thou, O Golden-crown,
Theban and named our own,
O Wine-gleam, Voice of Joy, for ever more
Ringed with thy Maenads white,
Bacchus, draw near and smite,
Smite with thy glad-eyed flame the God whom Gods abhor.

[During the last lines Oedipus has come out from the Palace.

Oedipus.

Thou prayest: but my words if thou wilt hear
And bow thee to their judgement, strength is near
For help, and a great lightening of ill.
Thereof I come to speak, a stranger still
To all this tale, a stranger to the deed:
(Else, save that I were clueless, little need
Had I to cast my net so wide and far:)
Howbeit, I, being now as all ye are,
A Theban, to all Thebans high and low
Do make proclaim: if any here doth know
By what man's hand died Laïus, your King,
Labdacus' son, I charge him that he bring
To me his knowledge. Let him feel no fear
If on a townsman's body he must clear
Our guilt: the man shall suffer no great ill,
But pass from Thebes, and live where else he will.

[No answer.

Is it some alien from an alien shore
Ye know to have done the deed, screen him no more!
Good guerdon waits you now and a King's love
Hereafter.

Hah! If still ye will not move
But, fearing for yourselves or some near friend,

Reject my charge, then hearken to what end
Ye drive me.—If in this place men there be
Who know and speak not, lo, I make decree
That, while in Thebes I bear the diadem,
No man shall greet, no man shall shelter them,
Nor give them water in their thirst, nor share
In sacrifice nor shrift nor dying prayer,
But thrust them from our doors, the thing they hide
Being this land's curse. Thus hath the God replied
This day to me from Delphi, and my sword
I draw thus for the dead and for God's word.
And lastly for the murderer, be it one
Hiding alone or more in unison,
I speak on him this curse: even as his soul
Is foul within him let his days be foul,
And life unfriended grind him till he die.
More: if he ever tread my hearth and I
Know it, be every curse upon my head
That I have spoke this day.
All I have said
I charge ye strictly to fulfil and make
Perfect, for my sake, for Apollo's sake,
And this land's sake, deserted of her fruit
And cast out from her gods. Nay, were all mute

At Delphi, still 'twere strange to leave the thing
Unfollowed, when a true man and a King
Lay murdered. All should search. But I, as now
Our fortunes fall—his crown is on my brow,
His wife lies in my arms, and common fate,
Had but his issue been more fortunate,
Might well have joined our children—since this red
Chance hath so stamped its heel on Laïus' head,
I am his champion left, and, as I would
For mine own father, choose for ill or good
This quest, to find the man who slew of yore
Labdacus' son, the son of Polydore,
Son of great Cadmus whom Agenor old
Begat, of Thebes first master. And, behold,
For them that aid me not, I pray no root
Nor seed in earth may bear them corn nor fruit,
No wife bear children, but this present curse
Cleave to them close and other woes yet worse.
Enough: ye other people of the land,
Whose will is one with mine, may Justice stand
Your helper, and all gods for evermore.

[The crowd disperses.

LEADER.

O King, even while thy curse yet hovers o'er
My head, I answer thee. I slew him not,
Nor can I shew the slayer. But, God wot,
If Phoebus sends this charge, let Phoebus read
Its meaning and reveal who did the deed.

OEDIPUS.

Aye, that were just, if of his grace he would
Reveal it. How shall man compel his God?

LEADER.

Second to that, methinks, 'twould help us most ...

OEDIPUS.

Though it be third, speak! Nothing should be lost.

LEADER.

To our High Seer on earth vision is given
Most like to that High Phoebus hath in heaven.
Ask of Tiresias: he could tell thee true.

OEDIPUS.

That also have I thought for. Aye, and two
Heralds have sent ere now. 'Twas Creon set
Me on.—I marvel that he comes not yet.

LEADER.

Our other clues are weak, old signs and far.

OEDIPUS.

What signs? I needs must question all that are.

LEADER.

Some travellers slew him, the tale used to be.

OEDIPUS.

The tale, yes: but the witness, where is he?

LEADER.

The man hath heard thy curses. If he knows
The taste of fear, he will not long stay close.

OEDIPUS.

He fear my words, who never feared the deed?

LEADER.

Well, there is one shall find him.—See, they lead
Hither our Lord Tiresias, in whose mind
All truth is born, alone of human kind.

Enter **TIRESIAS** *led by a young disciple. He is an old blind man in a prophet's robe, dark, unkempt and sinister in appearance.*

OEDIPUS.

Tiresias, thou whose mind divineth well
All Truth, the spoken and the unspeakable,

The things of heaven and them that walk the earth;
Our city ... thou canst see, for all thy dearth
Of outward eyes, what clouds are over her.
In which, O gracious Lord, no minister
Of help, no champion, can we find at all
Save thee. For Phoebus—thou hast heard withal
His message—to our envoy hath decreed
One only way of help in this great need:
To find and smite with death or banishing,
Him who smote Laïus, our ancient King.
Oh, grudge us nothing! Question every cry
Of birds, and all roads else of prophecy
Thou knowest. Save our city: save thine own
Greatness: save me; save all that yet doth groan
Under the dead man's wrong! Lo, in thy hand
We lay us. And, methinks, no work so grand
Hath man yet compassed, as, with all he can
Of chance or power, to help his fellow man.

TIRESIAS (*to himself*).

Ah me!
A fearful thing is knowledge, when to know
Helpeth no end. I knew this long ago,
But crushed it dead. Else had I never come.

OEDIPUS.

What means this? Comest thou so deep in gloom?

TIRESIAS.

Let me go back! Thy work shall weigh on thee
The less, if thou consent, and mine on me.

OEDIPUS.

Prophet, this is not lawful; nay, nor kind
To Thebes, who feeds thee, thus to veil thy mind.

TIRESIAS.

'Tis that I like not thy mind, nor the way
It goeth. Therefore, lest I also stray....

[He moves to go off. OEDIPUS *bars his road.*

OEDIPUS.

Thou shalt not, knowing, turn and leave us! See,
We all implore thee, all, on bended knee.

TIRESIAS.

All without light!—And never light shall shine
On this dark evil that is mine ... and thine.

OEDIPUS.

What wilt thou? Know and speak not? In my need
Be false to me, and let thy city bleed?

TIRESIAS.

I will not wound myself nor thee. Why seek
To trap and question me? I will not speak.

OEDIPUS.

Thou devil!

[Movement of LEADER *to check him.*

Nay; the wrath of any stone
Would rise at him. It lies with thee to have done
And speak. Is there no melting in thine eyes!

TIRESIAS.

Naught lies with me! With thee, with thee there lies,
I warrant, what thou ne'er hast seen nor guessed.

OEDIPUS (*to Leader, who tries to calm him.*)

How can I hear such talk?—he maketh jest
Of the land's woe—and keep mine anger dumb?

TIRESIAS.

Howe'er I hold it back, 'twill come, 'twill come.

OEDIPUS.

The more shouldst thou declare it to thy King.

TIRESIAS.

I speak no more. For thee, if passioning
Doth comfort thee, on, passion to thy fill!

[He moves to go.

OEDIPUS.

'Fore God, I am in wrath; and speak I will,
Nor stint what I see clear. 'Twas thou, 'twas thou,
Didst plan this murder; aye, and, save the blow,
Wrought it.—I know thou art blind; else I could swear
Thou, and thou only, art the murderer.

TIRESIAS (*returning*).

So?—I command thee by thine own word's power,
To stand accurst, and never from this hour
Speak word to me, nor yet to these who ring
Thy throne. Thou art thyself the unclean thing.

OEDIPUS.

Thou front of brass, to fling out injury
So wild! Dost think to bate me and go free?

TIRESIAS.

I am free. The strong truth is in this heart.

OEDIPUS.

What prompted thee? I swear 'twas not thine art.

TIRESIAS.

'Twas thou. I spoke not, save for thy command.

OEDIPUS.

Spoke what? What was it? Let me understand.

TIRESIAS.

Dost tempt me? Were my words before not plain!

OEDIPUS.

Scarce thy full meaning. Speak the words again.

TIRESIAS.

Thou seek'st this man of blood: Thyself art he.

OEDIPUS.

'Twill cost thee dear, twice to have stabbed at me!

TIRESIAS.

Shall I say more, to see thee rage again?

OEDIPUS.

Oh, take thy fill of speech: 'twill all be vain.

TIRESIAS.

Thou livest with those near to thee in shame

Most deadly, seeing not thyself nor them.

OEDIPUS.

Thou think'st 'twill help thee, thus to speak and speak?

TIRESIAS.

Surely, until the strength of Truth be weak.

OEDIPUS.

'Tis weak to none save thee. Thou hast no part

In truth, thou blind man, blind eyes, ears and heart.

TIRESIAS.

More blind, more sad thy words of scorn, which none
Who hears but shall cast back on thee: soon, soon.

OEDIPUS.

Thou spawn of Night, not I nor any free
And seeing man would hurt a thing like thee.

TIRESIAS.

God is enough.—'Tis not my doom to fall
By thee. He knows and shall accomplish all.

OEDIPUS (*with a flash of discovery*).

Ha! Creon!—Is it his or thine, this plot?

TIRESIAS.

'Tis thyself hates thee. Creon hates thee not.

OEDIPUS.

O wealth and majesty, O conquering skill
That carved life's rebel pathways to my will,
What is your heart but bitterness, if now
For this poor crown Thebes bound upon my brow,
A gift, a thing I sought not—for this crown
Creon the stern and true, Creon mine own
Comrade, comes creeping in the dark to ban

And slay me; sending first this magic-man
And schemer, this false beggar-priest, whose eye
Is bright for gold and blind for prophecy?
Speak, thou. When hast thou ever shown thee strong
For aid? The She-Wolf of the woven song
Came, and thy art could find no word, no breath,
To save thy people from her riddling death.
'Twas scarce a secret, that, for common men
To unravel. There was need of Seer-craft then.
And thou hadst none to show. No fowl, no flame,
No God revealed it thee. 'Twas I that came,
Rude Oedipus, unlearned in wizard's lore,
And read her secret, and she spoke no more.
Whom now thou thinkest to hunt out, and stand
Foremost in honour at King Creon's hand.
I think ye will be sorry, thou and he
That shares thy sin-hunt. Thou dost look to me
An old man; else, I swear this day should bring
On thee the death thou plottest for thy King.

LEADER.

Lord Oedipus, these be but words of wrath,
All thou hast spoke and all the Prophet hath.
Which skills not. We must join, for ill or well,

In search how best to obey God's oracle.

TIRESIAS.

King though thou art, thou needs must bear the right
Of equal answer. Even in me is might
For thus much, seeing I live no thrall of thine,
But Lord Apollo's; neither do I sign
Where Creon bids me.
I am blind, and thou
Hast mocked my blindness. Yea, I will speak now.
Eyes hast thou, but thy deeds thou canst not see
Nor where thou art, nor what things dwell with thee.
Whence art thou born? Thou know'st not; and unknown,
On quick and dead, on all that were thine own,
Thou hast wrought hate. For that across thy path
Rising, a mother's and a father's wrath,
Two-handed, shod with fire, from the haunts of men
Shall scourge thee, in thine eyes now light, but then
Darkness. Aye, shriek! What harbour of the sea,
What wild Kithairon shall not cry to thee
In answer, when thou hear'st what bridal song,
What wind among the torches, bore thy strong
Sail to its haven, not of peace but blood.
Yea, ill things multitude on multitude

Thou seest not, which so soon shall lay thee low,

Low as thyself, low as thy children.—Go,

Heap scorn on Creon and my lips withal:

For this I tell thee, never was there fall

Of pride, nor shall be, like to thine this day.

OEDIPUS.

To brook such words from this thing? Out, I say!

Out to perdition! Aye, and quick, before ...

[The LEADER *restrains him.*

Enough then!—Turn and get thee from my door.

TIRESIAS.

I had not come hadst thou not called me here.

OEDIPUS.

I knew thee not so dark a fool. I swear

'Twere long before I called thee, had I known.

TIRESIAS.

Fool, say'st thou? Am I truly such an one?

The two who gave thee birth, they held me wise.

OEDIPUS.

Birth?... Stop! Who were they? Speak thy prophecies.

TIRESIAS.

This day shall give thee birth and blot thee out.

OEDIPUS.

Oh, riddles everywhere and words of doubt!

TIRESIAS.

Aye. Thou wast their best reader long ago.

OEDIPUS.

Laugh on. I swear thou still shalt find me so.

TIRESIAS.

That makes thy pride and thy calamity.

OEDIPUS.

I have saved this land, and care not if I die.

TIRESIAS.

Then I will go.—Give me thine arm, my child.

OEDIPUS.

Aye, help him quick.—To see him there makes wild

My heart. Once gone, he will not vex me more.

TIRESIAS *(turning again as he goes)*.

I fear thee not; nor will I go before

That word be spoken which I came to speak.

How canst thou ever touch me?—Thou dost seek

With threats and loud proclaim the man whose hand

Slew Laïus. Lo, I tell thee, he doth stand

Here. He is called a stranger, but these days

Shall prove him Theban true, nor shall he praise

His birthright. Blind, who once had seeing eyes,

Beggared, who once had riches, in strange guise,

His staff groping before him, he shall crawl

O'er unknown earth, and voices round him call:

"Behold the brother-father of his own

Children, the seed, the sower and the sown,

Shame to his mother's blood, and to his sire

Son, murderer, incest-worker."

Cool thine ire

With thought of these, and if thou find that aught

Faileth, then hold my craft a thing of naught.

[He goes out. Oedipus returns to the Palace.

CHORUS.

[They sing of the unknown murderer,

What man, what man is he whom the voice of Delphi's cell

Hath named of the bloody hand, of the deed no tongue may tell?

Let him fly, fly, for his need

Hath found him; oh, where is the speed

That flew with the winds of old, the team of North-Wind's spell?

For feet there be that follow. Yea, thunder-shod

And girt with fire he cometh, the Child of God;

And with him are they that fail not, the Sin-Hounds risen from Hell.

For the mountain hath spoken, a voice hath flashed from amid the snows,

That the wrath of the world go seek for the man whom no man knows.
Is he fled to the wild forest,
To caves where the eagles nest?
O angry bull of the rocks, cast out from thy herd-fellows!
Rage in his heart, and rage across his way,
He toileth ever to beat from his ears away
The word that floateth about him, living, where'er he goes.

[And of the Prophet's strange accusation.

Yet strange, passing strange, the wise augur and his lore;
And my heart it cannot speak; I deny not nor assent,
But float, float in wonder at things after and before;
Did there lie between their houses some old wrath unspent,
That Corinth against Cadmus should do murder by the way?
No tale thereof they tell, nor no sign thereof they show;
Who dares to rise for vengeance and cast Oedipus away
For a dark, dark death long ago!
Ah, Zeus knows, and Apollo, what is dark to mortal eyes;
They are Gods. But a prophet, hath he vision more than mine?
Who hath seen? Who can answer? There be wise men and unwise.
I will wait, I will wait, for the proving of the sign.
But I list not nor hearken when they speak Oedipus ill.
We saw his face of yore, when the riddling singer passed;
And we knew him that he loved us, and we saw him great in skill.
Oh, my heart shall uphold him to the last!

Enter CREON.

CREON.

Good brother citizens, a frantic word
I hear is spoken by our chosen Lord
Oedipus against me, and here am come
Indignant. If he dreams, 'mid all this doom
That weighs upon us, he hath had from me
Or deed or lightest thought of injury, ...
'Fore God, I have no care to see the sun
Longer with such a groaning name. Not one
Wound is it, but a multitude, if now
All Thebes must hold me guilty—aye, and thou
And all who loved me—of a deed so foul.

LEADER.

If words were spoken, it was scarce the soul
That spoke them: 'twas some sudden burst of wrath.

CREON.

The charge was made, then, that Tiresias hath
Made answer false, and that I bribed him, I?

LEADER.

It was—perchance for jest. I know not why.

CREON.

His heart beat true, his eyes looked steadily

And fell not, laying such a charge on me?

LEADER.

I know not. I have no eyes for the thing

My masters do.—But see, here comes the King.

Enter Oedipus from the Palace.

OEDIPUS.

How now, assassin? Walking at my gate

With eye undimmed, thou plotter demonstrate

Against this life, and robber of my crown?

God help thee! Me! What was it set me down

Thy butt? So dull a brain hast found in me

Aforetime, such a faint heart, not to see

Thy work betimes, or seeing not to smite?

Art thou not rash, this once! It needeth might

Of friends, it needeth gold, to make a throne

Thy quarry; and I fear me thou hast none.

CREON.

One thing alone I ask thee. Let me speak

As thou hast spoken; then, with knowledge, wreak

Thy judgement. I accept it without fear.

OEDIPUS.

More skill hast thou to speak than I to hear

Thee. There is peril found in thee and hate.

Creon.

That one thing let me answer ere too late.

Oedipus.

One thing be sure of, that thy plots are known.

Creon.

The man who thinks that bitter pride alone
Can guide him, without thought—his mind is sick.

Oedipus.

Who thinks to slay his brother with a trick
And suffer not himself, his eyes are blind.

Creon.

Thy words are more than just. But say what kind
Of wrong thou fanciest I have done thee. Speak.

Oedipus.

Didst urge me, or didst urge me not, to seek
A counsel from that man of prophecies?

Creon.

So judged I then, nor now judge otherwise.

Oedipus.

[Suddenly seeing a mode of attack.

How many years have passed since Laïus ...

[The words seem to choke him.

CREON.

Speak on. I cannot understand thee thus.

OEDIPUS.

[With an effort.

Passed in that bloody tempest from men's sight?

CREON.

Long years and old. I scarce can tell them right.

OEDIPUS.

At that time was this seer in Thebes, or how?

CREON.

He was; most wise and honoured, even as now.

OEDIPUS.

At that time did he ever speak my name?

CREON.

No. To mine ear at least it never came.

OEDIPUS.

Held you no search for those who slew your King?

CREON.

For sure we did, but found not anything.

OEDIPUS.

How came the all-knowing seer to leave it so?

CREON.

Ask him! I speak not where I cannot know.

OEDIPUS.

One thing thou canst, with knowledge full, I wot.

CREON.

Speak it. If true, I will conceal it not.

OEDIPUS.

This: that until he talked with thee, the seer

Ne'er spoke of me as Laïus' murderer.

CREON.

I know not if he hath so spoken now.

I heard him not.—But let me ask and thou

Answer me true, as I have answered thee.

OEDIPUS.

Ask, ask! Thou shalt no murder find in me.

CREON.

My sister is thy wife this many a day?

OEDIPUS.

That charge it is not in me to gainsay.

CREON.

Thou reignest, giving equal reign to her?

OEDIPUS.

Always to her desire I minister.

CREON.

Were we not all as one, she thou and I?

OEDIPUS.

Yes, thou false friend! There lies thy treachery.

CREON.

Not so! Nay, do but follow me and scan
Thine own charge close. Think'st thou that any man
Would rather rule and be afraid than rule
And sleep untroubled? Nay, where lives the fool—
I know them not nor am I one of them—
Who careth more to bear a monarch's name
Than do a monarch's deeds? As now I stand
All my desire I compass at thy hand.
Were I the King, full half my deeds were done
To obey the will of others, not mine own.
Were that as sweet, when all the tale were told,
As this calm griefless princedom that I hold
And silent power? Am I so blind of brain
That ease with glory tires me, and I fain
Must change them? All men now give me God-speed,
All smile to greet me. If a man hath need
Of thee, 'tis me he calleth to the gate,
As knowing that on my word hangs the fate

Of half he craves. Is life like mine a thing
To cast aside and plot to be a King?
Doth a sane man turn villain in an hour?
For me, I never lusted thus for power
Nor bore with any man who turned such lust
To doing.—But enough. I claim but just
Question. Go first to Pytho; find if well
And true I did report God's oracle.
Next, seek in Thebes for any plots entwined
Between this seer and me; which if ye find,
Then seize and strike me dead. Myself that day
Will sit with thee as judge and bid thee Slay!
But damn me not on one man's guess.—'Tis all
Unjust: to call a traitor true, to call
A true man traitor with no cause nor end!
And this I tell thee. He who plucks a friend
Out from his heart hath lost a treasured thing
Dear as his own dear life.
But Time shall bring
Truth back. 'Tis Time alone can make men know
What hearts are true; the false one day can show.

LEADER.

To one that fears to fall his words are wise,

O King; in thought the swift win not the prize.

OEDIPUS.

When he is swift who steals against my reign

With plots, then swift am I to plot again.

Wait patient, and his work shall have prevailed

Before I move, and mine for ever failed.

CREON.

How then? To banish me is thy intent?

OEDIPUS.

Death is the doom I choose, not banishment.

CREON.

Wilt never soften, never trust thy friend?

OEDIPUS.

First I would see how traitors meet their end.

CREON.

I see thou wilt not think.

OEDIPUS.

I think to save

My life.

CREON.

Think, too, of mine.

OEDIPUS.

Thine, thou born knave!

CREON.

Yes.... What, if thou art blind in everything?

OEDIPUS.

The King must be obeyed.

CREON.

Not if the King

Does evil.

OEDIPUS.

To your King! Ho, Thebes, mine own!

CREON.

Thebes is my country, not the King's alone.

[OEDIPUS *has drawn his sword; the* CHORUS *show signs of breaking into two parties to fight for* OEDIPUS *or for* CREON, *when the door opens and* JOCASTA *appears on the steps.*

LEADER.

Stay, Princes, stay! See, on the Castle stair

The Queen Jocasta standeth. Show to her

Your strife. She will assuage it as is well.

JOCASTA.

Vain men, what would ye with this angry swell

Of words heart-blinded? Is there in your eyes
No pity, thus, when all our city lies
Bleeding, to ply your privy hates?... Alack,
My lord, come in!—Thou, Creon, get thee back
To thine own house. And stir not to such stress
Of peril griefs that are but nothingness.

CREON.

Sister, it is the pleasure of thy lord,
Our King, to do me deadly wrong. His word
Is passed on me: 'tis banishment or death.

OEDIPUS.

I found him ... I deny not what he saith,
My Queen ... with craft and malice practising
Against my life.

CREON.

Ye Gods, if such a thing
Hath once been in my thoughts, may I no more
See any health on earth, but, festered o'er
With curses, die!—Have done. There is mine oath.

JOCASTA.

In God's name, Oedipus, believe him, both
For my sake, and for these whose hearts are all

Thine own, and for my brother's oath withal.

LEADER.*[Strophe.*

Yield; consent; think! My Lord, I conjure thee!

OEDIPUS.

What would ye have me do?

LEADER.

Reject not one who never failed his troth

Of old and now is strong in his great oath.

OEDIPUS.

Dost know what this prayer means?

LEADER.

Yea, verily!

OEDIPUS.

Say then the meaning true.

LEADER.

I would not have thee cast to infamy

Of guilt, where none is proved,

One who hath sworn and whom thou once hast loved.

OEDIPUS.

'Tis that ye seek? For me, then ... understand

Well ... ye seek death or exile from the land.

LEADER.

No, by the God of Gods, the all-seeing Sun!
May he desert me here, and every friend
With him, to death and utterest malison,
If e'er my heart could dream of such an end!
But it bleedeth, it bleedeth sore,
In a land half slain,
If we join to the griefs of yore
Griefs of you twain.

OEDIPUS.

Oh, let him go, though it be utterly
My death, or flight from Thebes in beggary.
'Tis thy sad lips, not his, that make me know
Pity. Him I shall hate, where'er he go.

CREON.

I see thy mercy moving full of hate
And slow; thy wrath came swift and desperate.
Methinks, of all the pain that such a heart
Spreadeth, itself doth bear the bitterest part.

OEDIPUS.

Oh, leave me and begone!

CREON.

I go, wronged sore

By thee. These friends will trust me as before.

*[*CREON *goes. Oedipus stands apart lost in trouble of mind.*

LEADER.*[Antistrophe.*

Queen, wilt thou lead him to his house again?

JOCASTA.

I will, when I have heard.

LEADER.

There fell some word, some blind imagining

Between them. Things known foolish yet can sting.

JOCASTA.

From both the twain it rose?

LEADER.

From both the twain.

JOCASTA.

Aye, and what was the word?

LEADER.

Surely there is enough of evil stirred,

And Thebes heaves on the swell

Of storm.—Oh, leave this lying where it fell.

OEDIPUS.

So be it, thou wise counsellor! Make slight

My wrong, and blunt my purpose ere it smite.

LEADER.

O King, not once I have answered. Visibly

Mad were I, lost to all wise usages,

To seek to cast thee from us. 'Twas from thee

We saw of old blue sky and summer seas,

When Thebes in the storm and rain

Reeled, like to die.

Oh, if thou canst, again

Blue sky, blue sky...!

JOCASTA.

Husband, in God's name, say what hath ensued

Of ill, that thou shouldst seek so dire a feud.

OEDIPUS.

I will, wife. I have more regard for thee

Than these.—Thy brother plots to murder me.

JOCASTA.

Speak on. Make all thy charge. Only be clear.

OEDIPUS.

He says that I am Laïus' murderer.

JOCASTA.

Says it himself? Says he hath witnesses?

Oedipus.

Nay, of himself he ventures nothing. 'Tis
This priest, this hellish seer, makes all the tale.

Jocasta.

The seer?—Then tear thy terrors like a veil
And take free breath. A seer? No human thing
Born on the earth hath power for conjuring
Truth from the dark of God.

Come, I will tell
An old tale. There came once an oracle
To Laïus: I say not from the God
Himself, but from the priests and seers who trod
His sanctuary: if ever son were bred
From him and me, by that son's hand, it said,
Laïus must die. And he, the tale yet stays
Among us, at the crossing of three ways
Was slain by robbers, strangers. And my son—
God's mercy!—scarcely the third day was gone
When Laïus took, and by another's hand
Out on the desert mountain, where the land
Is rock, cast him to die. Through both his feet
A blade of iron they drove. Thus did we cheat
Apollo of his will. My child could slay

No father, and the King could cast away

The fear that dogged him, by his child to die

Murdered.—Behold the fruits of prophecy!

Which heed not thou! God needs not that a seer

Help him, when he would make his dark things clear.

OEDIPUS.

Woman, what turmoil hath thy story wrought

Within me! What up-stirring of old thought!

JOCASTA.

What thought? It turns thee like a frightened thing.

OEDIPUS.

'Twas at the crossing of three ways this King

Was murdered? So I heard or so I thought.

JOCASTA.

That was the tale. It is not yet forgot.

OEDIPUS.

The crossing of three ways! And in what land?

JOCASTA.

Phokis 'tis called. A road on either hand

From Delphi comes and Daulia, in a glen.

OEDIPUS.

How many years and months have passed since then?

JOCASTA.

'Twas but a little time before proclaim
Was made of thee for king, the tidings came.

OEDIPUS.

My God, what hast thou willed to do with me?

JOCASTA.

Oedipus, speak! What is it troubles thee?

OEDIPUS.

Ask me not yet. But say, what build, what height
Had Laïus? Rode he full of youth and might?

JOCASTA.

Tall, with the white new gleaming on his brow
He walked. In shape just such a man as thou.

OEDIPUS.

God help me! I much fear that I have wrought
A curse on mine own head, and knew it not.

JOCASTA.

How sayst thou? O my King, I look on thee
And tremble.

OEDIPUS (to himself).

Horror, if the blind can see!
Answer but one thing and 'twill all be clear.

Jocasta.

Speak. I will answer though I shake with fear.

Oedipus.

Went he with scant array, or a great band
Of armèd followers, like a lord of land?

Jocasta.

Four men were with him, one a herald; one
Chariot there was, where Laïus rode alone.

Oedipus.

Aye me! Tis clear now.
Woman, who could bring
To Thebes the story of that manslaying?

Jocasta.

A house-thrall, the one man they failed to slay.

Oedipus.

The one man...? Is he in the house to-day?

Jocasta.

Indeed no. When he came that day, and found
Thee on the throne where once sat Laïus crowned,
He took my hand and prayed me earnestly
To send him to the mountain heights, to be
A herdsman, far from any sight or call

Of Thebes. And there I sent him. 'Twas a thrall
Good-hearted, worthy a far greater boon.

OEDIPUS.

Canst find him? I would see this herd, and soon.

JOCASTA.

'Tis easy. But what wouldst thou with the herd?

OEDIPUS.

I fear mine own voice, lest it spoke a word
Too much; whereof this man must tell me true.

JOCASTA.

The man shall come.—My lord, methinks I too
Should know what fear doth work thee this despite.

OEDIPUS.

Thou shalt. When I am tossed to such an height
Of dark foreboding, woman, when my mind
Faceth such straits as these, where should I find
A mightier love than thine?
My father—thus
I tell thee the whole tale—was Polybus,
In Corinth King; my mother Meropê
Of Dorian line. And I was held to be
The proudest in Corinthia, till one day
A thing befell: strange was it, but no way

Meet for such wonder and such rage as mine.
A feast it was, and some one flushed with wine
Cried out at me that I was no true son
Of Polybus. Oh, I was wroth! That one
Day I kept silence, but the morrow morn
I sought my parents, told that tale of scorn
And claimed the truth; and they rose in their pride
And smote the mocker.... Aye, they satisfied
All my desire; yet still the cavil gnawed
My heart, and still the story crept abroad.
At last I rose—my father knew not, nor
My mother—and went forth to Pytho's floor
To ask. And God in that for which I came
Rejected me, but round me, like a flame,
His voice flashed other answers, things of woe,
Terror, and desolation. I must know
My mother's body and beget thereon
A race no mortal eye durst look upon,
And spill in murder mine own father's blood.
I heard, and, hearing, straight from where I stood,
No landmark but the stars to light my way,
Fled, fled from the dark south where Corinth lay,
To lands far off, where never I might see
My doom of scorn fulfilled. On bitterly

I strode, and reached the region where, so saith
Thy tale, that King of Thebes was struck to death....
Wife, I will tell thee true. As one in daze
I walked, till, at the crossing of three ways,
A herald, like thy tale, and o'er his head
A man behind strong horses charioted
Met me. And both would turn me from the path,
He and a thrall in front. And I in wrath
Smote him that pushed me—'twas a groom who led
The horses. Not a word the master said,
But watched, and as I passed him on the road
Down on my head his iron-branchèd goad
Stabbed. But, by heaven, he rued it! In a flash
I swung my staff and saw the old man crash
Back from his car in blood.... Then all of them
I slew.
Oh, if that man's unspoken name
Had aught of Laïus in him, in God's eye
What man doth move more miserable than I,
More dogged by the hate of heaven! No man, kin
Nor stranger, any more may take me in;
No man may greet me with a word, but all
Cast me from out their houses. And withal
'Twas mine own self that laid upon my life

These curses.—And I hold the dead man's wife
In these polluting arms that spilt his soul....
Am I a thing born evil? Am I foul
In every vein? Thebes now doth banish me,
And never in this exile must I see
Mine ancient folk of Corinth, never tread
The land that bore me; else my mother's bed
Shall be defiled, and Polybus, my good
Father, who loved me well, be rolled in blood.
If one should dream that such a world began
In some slow devil's heart, that hated man,
Who should deny him?—God, as thou art clean,
Suffer not this, oh, suffer not this sin
To be, that e'er I look on such a day!
Out of all vision of mankind away
To darkness let me fall ere such a fate
Touch me, so unclean and so desolate!

Leader.

I tremble too, O King; but till thou hear
From him who saw, oh, let hope conquer fear.

Oedipus.

One shred of hope I still have, and therefore
Will wait the herdsman's coming. 'Tis no more.

JOCASTA.

He shall come. But what further dost thou seek?

OEDIPUS.

This. If we mark him close and find him speak
As thou hast, then I am lifted from my dread.

JOCASTA.

What mean'st thou? Was there something that I said...?

OEDIPUS.

Thou said'st he spoke of robbers, a great band,
That slaughtered Laïus' men. If still he stand
To the same tale, the guilt comes not my way.
One cannot be a band. But if he say
One lonely loin-girt man, then visibly
This is God's finger pointing toward me.

JOCASTA.

Be sure of this. He told the story so
When first he came. All they that heard him know,
Not only I. He cannot change again
Now. And if change he should, O Lord of men,
No change of his can make the prophecy
Of Laïus' death fall true. He was to die
Slain by my son. So Loxias spake.... My son!
He slew no man, that poor deserted one

That died.... And I will no more turn mine eyes

This way nor that for all their prophecies.

OEDIPUS.

Woman, thou counsellest well. Yet let it not

Escape thee. Send and have the herdsman brought.

JOCASTA.

That will I.—Come. Thou knowest I ne'er would do

Nor think of aught, save thou wouldst have it so.

*[***JOCASTA*** and ***OEDIPUS*** go together into the Palace.*

CHORUS.

[They pray to be free from such great sins as they have just heard spoken of.

[Strophe.

Toward God's great mysteries, oh, let me move

Unstainèd till I die

In speech or doing; for the Laws thereof

Are holy, walkers upon ways above,

Born in the far blue sky;

Their father is Olympus uncreate;

No man hath made nor told

Their being; neither shall Oblivion set

Sleep on their eyes, for in them lives a great

Spirit and grows not old.[Antistrophe.

[They wonder if these sins be all due to pride and if Creon has guilty ambitions;

'Tis Pride that breeds the tyrant; drunken deep

With perilous things is she,

Which bring not peace: up, reeling, steep on steep

She climbs, till lo, the rock-edge, and the leap

To that which needs must be,

The land where the strong foot is no more strong!

Yet is there surely Pride

That saves a city; God preserve it long!

I judge not. Only through all maze of wrong

Be God, not man, my guide.*[Strophe.*

[Or if Tiresias can really be a lying prophet with no fear of God; they feel that all faith in oracles and the things of God is shaken.

Is there a priest who moves amid the altars

Ruthless in deed and word,

Fears not the presence of his god, nor falters

Lest Right at last be heard?

If such there be, oh, let some doom be given

Meet for his ill-starred pride,

Who will not gain his gain where Justice is,

Who will not hold his lips from blasphemies,

Who hurls rash hands amid the things of heaven

From man's touch sanctified.

In a world where such things be,

What spirit hath shield or lance

To ward him secretly

From the arrow that slays askance?

If honour to such things be,

Why should I dance my dance?

[Antistrophe.

I go no more with prayers and adorations

To Earth's deep Heart of Stone,

Nor yet the Abantes' floor, nor where the nations

Kneel at Olympia's throne,

Till all this dark be lightened, for the finger

Of man to touch and know.

O Thou that rulest—if men rightly call

Thy name on earth—O Zeus, thou Lord of all

And Strength undying, let not these things linger

Unknown, tossed to and fro.

For faint is the oracle,

And they thrust it aside, away;

And no more visible

Apollo to save or slay;

And the things of God, they fail

As mist on the wind away.

[Jocasta comes out from the Palace followed by handmaids bearing incense and flowers.

JOCASTA.

Lords of the land, the ways my thought hath trod
Lead me in worship to these shrines of God
With flowers and incense flame. So dire a storm
Doth shake the King, sin, dread and every form
Of grief the world knows. 'Tis the wise man's way
To judge the morrow by the yesterday;
Which he doth never, but gives eye and ear
To all who speak, will they but speak of fear.
And seeing no word of mine hath power to heal
His torment, therefore forth to thee I steal,
O Slayer of the Wolf, O Lord of Light,
Apollo: thou art near us, and of right
Dost hold us thine: to thee in prayer I fall.
[She kneels at the altar of Apollo Lukeios.
Oh, show us still some path that is not all
Unclean; for now our captain's eyes are dim
With dread, and the whole ship must follow him.

[While she prays a Stranger has entered and begins to accost the Chorus.

STRANGER.

Good masters, is there one of you could bring
My steps to the house of Oedipus, your King?
Or, better, to himself if that may be?

LEADER.

This is the house and he within; and she
Thou seest, the mother of his royal seed.
[Jocasta rises, anxious, from her prayer.

STRANGER.

Being wife to such a man, happy indeed
And ringed with happy faces may she live!

JOCASTA.

To one so fair of speech may the Gods give
Like blessing, courteous stranger; 'tis thy due.
But say what leads thee hither. Can we do
Thy wish in aught, or hast thou news to bring?

STRANGER.

Good news, O Queen, for thee and for the King.

JOCASTA.

What is it? And from what prince comest thou?

STRANGER.

I come from Corinth.—And my tale, I trow,

Will give thee joy, yet haply also pain.

JOCASTA.

What news can have that twofold power? Be plain.

STRANGER.

'Tis spoke in Corinth that the gathering

Of folk will make thy lord our chosen King.

JOCASTA.

How? Is old Polybus in power no more?

STRANGER.

Death has a greater power. His reign is o'er.

JOCASTA.

What say'st thou? Dead?... Oedipus' father dead?

STRANGER.

If I speak false, let me die in his stead.

JOCASTA.

Ho, maiden! To our master! Hie thee fast

And tell this tale.

[The maiden goes.

Where stand ye at the last

Ye oracles of God? For many a year

Oedipus fled before that man, in fear

To slay him. And behold we find him thus

Slain by a chance death, not by Oedipus.

[Oedipus comes out from the Palace.

OEDIPUS.

O wife, O face I love to look upon,

Why call'st thou me from where I sat alone?

JOCASTA.

Give ear, and ponder from what this man tells

How end these proud priests and their oracles.

OEDIPUS.

Whence comes he? And what word hath he for us?

JOCASTA.

From Corinth; bearing news that Polybus

Thy father is no more. He has found his death.

OEDIPUS.

How?—Stranger, speak thyself. This that she saith ...

STRANGER.

Is sure. If that is the first news ye crave,

I tell thee, Polybus lieth in his grave.

OEDIPUS.

Not murdered?... How? Some passing of disease?

STRANGER.

A slight thing turns an old life to its peace.

OEDIPUS.

Poor father!... 'Tis by sickness he is dead?

STRANGER.

The growing years lay heavy on his head.

OEDIPUS.

O wife, why then should man fear any more
The voice of Pytho's dome, or cower before
These birds that shriek above us? They foretold
Me for my father's murderer; and behold,
He lies in Corinth dead, and here am I
And never touched the sword.... Or did he die
In grief for me who left him? In that way
I may have wrought his death.... But come what may,
He sleepeth in his grave and with him all
This deadly seercraft, of no worth at all.

JOCASTA.

Dear Lord, long since did I not show thee clear...?

OEDIPUS.

Indeed, yes. I was warped by mine own fear.

JOCASTA.

Now thou wilt cast it from thee, and forget.

OEDIPUS.

Forget my mother?... It is not over yet.

JOCASTA.

What should man do with fear, who hath but Chance
Above him, and no sight nor governance
Of things to be? To live as life may run,
No fear, no fret, were wisest 'neath the sun.
And thou, fear not thy mother. Prophets deem
A deed wrought that is wrought but in a dream.
And he to whom these things are nothing, best
Will bear his burden.

OEDIPUS.

All thou counsellest
Were good, save that my mother liveth still.
And, though thy words be wise, for good or ill
Her I still fear.

JOCASTA.

Think of thy father's tomb!
Like light across our darkness it hath come.

OEDIPUS.

Great light; but while she lives I fly from her.

STRANGER.

What woman, Prince, doth fill thee so with fear?

OEDIPUS.

Meropê, friend, who dwelt with Polybus.

STRANGER.

What in Queen Meropê should fright thee thus?

OEDIPUS.

A voice of God, stranger, of dire import.

STRANGER.

Meet for mine ears? Or of some secret sort?

OEDIPUS.

Nay, thou must hear, and Corinth. Long ago
Apollo spake a doom, that I should know
My mother's flesh, and with mine own hand spill
My father's blood.—'Tis that, and not my will,
Hath kept me always far from Corinth. So;
Life hath dealt kindly with me, yet men know
On earth no comfort like a mother's face.

STRANGER.

'Tis that, hath kept thee exiled in this place?

OEDIPUS.

That, and the fear too of my father's blood.

STRANGER.

Then, surely, Lord ... I came but for thy good ...

'Twere well if from that fear I set thee free.

OEDIPUS.

Ah, couldst thou! There were rich reward for thee.

STRANGER.

To say truth, I had hoped to lead thee home

Now, and myself to get some good therefrom.

OEDIPUS.

Nay; where my parents are I will not go.

STRANGER.

My son, 'tis very clear thou dost not know

What road thou goest.

OEDIPUS.

How? In God's name, say!

How clear?

STRANGER.

'Tis this, keeps thee so long away

From Corinth?

OEDIPUS.

'Tis the fear lest that word break

One day upon me true.

STRANGER.

Fear lest thou take

Defilement from the two that gave thee birth?

OEDIPUS.

'Tis that, old man, 'tis that doth fill the earth

With terror.

STRANGER.

Then thy terror all hath been

For nothing.

OEDIPUS.

How? Were not your King and Queen

My parents?

STRANGER.

Polybus was naught to thee

In blood.

OEDIPUS.

How? He, my father!

STRANGER.

That was he

As much as I, but no more.

OEDIPUS.

Thou art naught;

'Twas he begot me.

Stranger.

'Twas not I begot
Oedipus, neither was it he.

Oedipus.

What wild
Fancy, then, made him name me for his child?

Stranger.

Thou wast his child—by gift. Long years ago
Mine own hand brought thee to him.

Oedipus.

Coming so,
From a strange hand, he gave me that great love?

Stranger.

He had no child, and the desire thereof
Held him.

Oedipus.

And thou didst find somewhere—or buy—
A child for him?

Stranger.

I found it in a high
Glen of Kithairon.

[Movement of JOCASTA*, who stands riveted with dread, unnoticed by the others.*

OEDIPUS.

Yonder? To what end

Wast travelling in these parts?

STRANGER.

I came to tend

The flocks here on the mountain.

OEDIPUS.

Thou wast one

That wandered, tending sheep for hire?

STRANGER.

My son,

That day I was the saviour of a King.

OEDIPUS.

How saviour? Was I in some suffering Or peril?

STRANGER.

Thine own feet a tale could speak.

OEDIPUS.

Ah me! What ancient pain stirs half awake Within me!

STRANGER.

'Twas a spike through both thy feet.

I set thee free.

OEDIPUS.

A strange scorn that, to greet

A babe new on the earth!

STRANGER.

From that they fain

Must call thee Oedipus, "*Who-walks-in-pain.*"

OEDIPUS.

Who called me so—father or mother? Oh,

In God's name, speak!

STRANGER.

I know not. He should know

Who brought thee.

OEDIPUS.

So: I was not found by thee.

Thou hadst me from another?

STRANGER.

Aye; to me

One of the shepherds gave the babe, to bear

Far off.

OEDIPUS.

What shepherd? Know'st thou not? Declare

All that thou knowest.

STRANGER.

By my memory, then,

I think they called him one of Laïus' men.

OEDIPUS.

That Laïus who was king in Thebes of old?

STRANGER.

The same. My man did herding in his fold.

OEDIPUS.

Is he yet living? Can I see his face?

STRANGER.

[Turning to the Chorus.

Ye will know that, being natives to the place.

OEDIPUS.

How?—Is there one of you within my pale

Standing, that knows the shepherd of his tale?

Ye have seen him on the hills? Or in this town?

Speak! For the hour is come that all be known.

LEADER.

I think 'twill be the Peasant Man, the same,

Thou hast sought long time to see.—His place and name

Our mistress, if she will, can tell most clear.

*[*JOCASTA *remains as if she heard nothing.*

Oedipus.

Thou hear'st him, wife. The herd whose presence here

We craved for, is it he this man would say?

Jocasta.

He saith ... What of it? Ask not; only pray Not to remember.... Tales are vainly told.

Oedipus.

'Tis mine own birth. How can I, when I hold Such clues as these, refrain from knowing all?

Jocasta.

For God's love, no! Not if thou car'st at all For thine own life.... My anguish is enough.

Oedipus (*bitterly*).

Fear not!... Though I be thrice of slavish stuff

From my third grand-dam down, it shames not thee.

Jocasta.

Ask no more. I beseech thee.... Promise me!

Oedipus.

To leave the Truth half-found? 'Tis not my mood.

Jocasta.

I understand; and tell thee what is good.

Oedipus.

Thy good doth weary me.

JOCASTA.

O child of woe,

I pray God, I pray God, thou never know!

OEDIPUS (*turning from her*).

Go, fetch the herdsman straight!—This Queen of mine May walk alone to boast her royal line.

JOCASTA.

[She twice draws in her breath through her teeth, as if in some sharp pain.

Unhappy one, goodbye! Goodbye before

I go: this once, and never never more!

[She comes towards him as though to take a last farewell, then stops suddenly, turns, and rushes into the Palace.

LEADER.

King, what was that? She passed like one who flies

In very anguish. Dread is o'er mine eyes

Lest from this silence break some storm of wrong.

OEDIPUS.

Break what break will! My mind abideth strong

To know the roots, how low soe'er they be,

Which grew to Oedipus. This woman, she

Is proud, methinks, and fears my birth and name

Will mar her nobleness. But I, no shame

Can ever touch me. I am Fortune's child,

Not man's; her mother face hath ever smiled

Above me, and my brethren of the sky,

The changing Moons, have changed me low and high.

There is my lineage true, which none shall wrest

From me; who then am I to fear this quest?

CHORUS.

[They sing Oedipus as the foundling of their own Theban mountain, Kithairon, and doubtless of divine birth.

[Strophe.

If I, O Kithairon, some vision can borrow

From seercraft, if still there is wit in the old,

Long, long, through the deep-orbèd Moon of the morrow—

So hear me, Olympus!—thy tale shall be told.

O mountain of Thebes, a new Theban shall praise thee,

One born of thy bosom, one nursed at thy springs;

And the old men shall dance to thy glory, and raise thee

To worship, O bearer of joy to my kings.

And thou, we pray,

Look down in peace, O Apollo; I-ê, I-ê!

[Antistrophe.

What Oread mother, unaging, unweeping,

Did bear thee, O Babe, to the Crag-walker Pan;

Or perchance to Apollo? He loveth the leaping
Of herds on the rock-ways unhaunted of man.
Or was it the lord of Cyllênê, who found thee,
Or glad Dionysus, whose home is the height,
Who knew thee his own on the mountain, as round thee
The White Brides of Helicon laughed for delight?
'Tis there, 'tis there,
The joy most liveth of all his dance and prayer.

OEDIPUS.

If I may judge, ye Elders, who have ne'er
Seen him, methinks I see the shepherd there
Whom we have sought so long. His weight of years
Fits well with our Corinthian messenger's;
And, more, I know the men who guide his way,
Bondsmen of mine own house.
Thou, friend, wilt say
Most surely, who hast known the man of old.

LEADER.

I know him well. A shepherd of the fold
Of Laïus, one he trusted more than all.

[*The* SHEPHERD *comes in, led by two thralls. He is an old man and seems terrified.*

OEDIPUS.

Thou first, our guest from Corinth: say withal

Is this the man?

STRANGER.

This is the man, O King.

OEDIPUS.

[*Addressing the* SHEPHERD.

Old man! Look up, and answer everything

I ask thee.—Thou wast Laïus' man of old?

SHEPHERD.

Born in his house I was, not bought with gold.

OEDIPUS.

What kind of work, what way of life, was thine?

SHEPHERD.

Most of my days I tended sheep or kine.

OEDIPUS.

What was thy camping ground at midsummer?

SHEPHERD.

Sometimes Kithairon, sometimes mountains near.

OEDIPUS.

Saw'st ever there this man thou seëst now?

SHEPHERD.

There, Lord? What doing?—What man meanest thou?

OEDIPUS.

[Pointing to the Stranger.

Look! Hath he ever crossed thy path before?

SHEPHERD.

I call him not to mind, I must think more.

STRANGER.

Small wonder that, O King! But I will throw
Light on his memories.—Right well I know
He knows the time when, all Kithairon through,
I with one wandering herd and he with two,
Three times we neighboured one another, clear
From spring to autumn stars, a good half-year.
At winter's fall we parted; he drove down
To his master's fold, and I back to mine own....
Dost call it back, friend? Was it as I say?

SHEPHERD.

It was. It was.... 'Tis all so far away.

STRANGER.

Say then: thou gavest me once, there in the wild,
A babe to rear far off as mine own child?

SHEPHERD.

[His terror returning.

What does this mean? To what end askest thou?

STRANGER.

[Pointing to **OEDIPUS**.

That babe has grown, friend. 'Tis our master now.

SHEPHERD.

[He slowly understands, then stands for a moment horror-struck.

No, in the name of death!... Fool, hold thy peace.

[He lifts his staff at the Stranger.

OEDIPUS.

Ha, greybeard! Wouldst thou strike him?—'Tis not his

Offences, 'tis thine own we need to mend.

SHEPHERD.

Most gentle master, how do I offend?

OEDIPUS.

Whence came that babe whereof he questioneth?

SHEPHERD.

He doth not know ... 'tis folly ... what he saith.

OEDIPUS.

Thou wilt not speak for love; but pain maybe ...

SHEPHERD.

I am very old. Ye would not torture me.

OEDIPUS.

Back with his arms, ye bondmen! Hold him so.

[The thralls drag back the Shepherd's arms, ready for torture.

SHEPHERD.

Woe's me! What have I done?... What wouldst thou know?

OEDIPUS.

Didst give this man the child, as he doth say?

SHEPHERD.

I did.... Would God that I had died this day!

OEDIPUS.

'Fore heaven, thou shalt yet, if thou speak not true.

SHEPHERD.

'Tis more than death and darker, if I do.

OEDIPUS.

This dog, it seems, will keep us waiting.

SHEPHERD.

Nay,

I said at first I gave it.

OEDIPUS.

In what way

Came it to thee? Was it thine own child, or

Another's?

SHEPHERD.

Nay, it never crossed my door:

Another's.

OEDIPUS.

Whose? What man, what house, of these

About thee?

SHEPHERD.

In the name of God who sees,

Ask me no more!

OEDIPUS.

If once I ask again,

Thou diest.

SHEPHERD.

From the folk of Laïus, then,

It came.

OEDIPUS.

A slave, or born of Laïus' blood?

SHEPHERD.

There comes the word I dread to speak, O God!

OEDIPUS.

And I to hear: yet heard it needs must be.

SHEPHERD.

Know then, they said 'twas Laïus' child. But she

Within, thy wife, best knows its fathering.

OEDIPUS.

'Twas she that gave it?

SHEPHERD.

It was she, O King.

OEDIPUS.

And bade you ... what?

SHEPHERD.

Destroy it.

OEDIPUS.

Her own child?...

Cruel!

SHEPHERD.

Dark words of God had made her wild.

OEDIPUS.

What words?

SHEPHERD.

The babe must slay his father; so

'Twas written.

OEDIPUS.

Why didst thou, then, let him go

With this old man?

SHEPHERD.

O King, I pitied him.

I thought the man would save him to some dim

And distant land, beyond all fear.... And he,

To worse than death, did save him!... Verily,

If thou art he whom this man telleth of,

To sore affliction thou art born.

OEDIPUS.

Enough!

All, all, shall be fulfilled.... Oh, on these eyes

Shed light no more, ye everlasting skies

That know my sin! I have sinned in birth and breath.

I have sinned with Woman. I have sinned with Death.

[He rushes into the Palace. The Shepherd is led away by the thralls.

CHORUS.

[Strophe.

Nothingness, nothingness,

Ye Children of Man, and less

I count you, waking or dreaming!

And none among mortals, none,

Seeking to live, hath won

More than to seem, and to cease

Again from his seeming.

While ever before mine eyes

One fate, one ensample, lies—

Thine, thine, O Oedipus, sore

Of God oppressèd—

What thing that is human more

Dare I call blessèd?

[Antistrophe.

Straight his archery flew

To the heart of living; he knew

Joy and the fulness of power,

O Zeus, when the riddling breath

Was stayed and the Maid of Death

Slain, and we saw him through

The death-cloud, a tower!

For that he was called my king;

Yea, every precious thing

Wherewith men are honoured, down

We cast before him,

And great Thebes brought her crown

And kneeled to adore him.

[Strophe.

But now, what man's story is such bitterness to speak?

What life hath Delusion so visited, and Pain,

And swiftness of Disaster?

O great King, our master,

How oped the one haven to the slayer and the slain?

And the furrows of thy father, did they turn not nor shriek,

Did they bear so long silent thy casting of the grain?

[Antistrophe.

'Tis Time, Time, desireless, hath shown thee what thou art;

The long monstrous mating, it is judged and all its race.

O child of him that sleepeth,

Thy land weepeth, weepeth,

Unfathered.... Would God, I had never seen thy face!

From thee in great peril fell peace upon my heart,

In thee mine eye clouded and the dark is come apace.

[A Messenger rushes out from the Palace.

MESSENGER.

O ye above this land in honour old

Exalted, what a tale shall ye be told,

What sights shall see, and tears of horror shed,

If still your hearts be true to them that led

Your sires! There runs no river, well I ween,
Not Phasis nor great Ister, shall wash clean
This house of all within that hideth—nay,
Nor all that creepeth forth to front the day,
Of purposed horror. And in misery
That woundeth most which men have willed to be.

LEADER.

No lack there was in what we knew before
Of food for heaviness. What bring'st thou more?

MESSENGER.

One thing I bring thee first.... 'Tis quickly said.
Jocasta, our anointed queen, is dead.

LEADER.

Unhappy woman! How came death to her?

MESSENGER.

By her own hand.... Oh, of what passed in there
Ye have been spared the worst. Ye cannot see.
Howbeit, with that which still is left in me
Of mind and memory, ye shall hear her fate.
Like one entranced with passion, through the gate
She passed, the white hands flashing o'er her head,
Like blades that tear, and fled, unswerving fled,

Toward her old bridal room, and disappeared
And the doors crashed behind her. But we heard
Her voice within, crying to him of old,
Her Laïus, long dead; and things untold
Of the old kiss unforgotten, that should bring
The lover's death and leave the loved a thing
Of horror, yea, a field beneath the plough
For sire and son: then wailing bitter-low
Across that bed of births unreconciled,
Husband from husband born and child from child.
And, after that, I know not how her death
Found her. For sudden, with a roar of wrath,
Burst Oedipus upon us. Then, I ween,
We marked no more what passion held the Queen,
But him, as in the fury of his stride,
"A sword! A sword! And show me here," he cried,
"That wife, no wife, that field of bloodstained earth
Where husband, father, sin on sin, had birth,
Polluted generations!" While he thus
Raged on, some god—for sure 'twas none of us—
Showed where she was; and with a shout away,
As though some hand had pointed to the prey,
He dashed him on the chamber door. The straight
Door-bar of oak, it bent beneath his weight,

Shook from its sockets free, and in he burst
To the dark chamber.
There we saw her first
Hanged, swinging from a noose, like a dead bird.
He fell back when he saw her. Then we heard
A miserable groan, and straight he found
And loosed the strangling knot, and on the ground
Laid her.—Ah, then the sight of horror came!
The pin of gold, broad-beaten like a flame,
He tore from off her breast, and, left and right,
Down on the shuddering orbits of his sight
Dashed it: "Out! Out! Ye never more shall see
Me nor the anguish nor the sins of me.
Ye looked on lives whose like earth never bore,
Ye knew not those my spirit thirsted for:
Therefore be dark for ever!"
Like a song
His voice rose, and again, again, the strong
And stabbing hand fell, and the massacred
And bleeding eyeballs streamed upon his beard,
Wild rain, and gouts of hail amid the rain.
Behold affliction, yea, afflictions twain
From man and woman broken, now made one
In downfall. All the riches yester sun

Saw in this house were rich in verity.

What call ye now our riches? Agony,

Delusion, Death, Shame, all that eye or ear

Hath ever dreamed of misery, is here.

LEADER.

And now how fares he? Doth the storm abate?

MESSENGER.

He shouts for one to open wide the gate

And lead him forth, and to all Thebes display

His father's murderer, his mother's.... Nay,

Such words I will not speak. And his intent

Is set, to cast himself in banishment

Out to the wild, not walk 'mid human breed

Bearing the curse he bears. Yet sore his need

Of strength and of some guiding hand. For sure

He hath more burden now than man may endure.

But see, the gates fall back, and that appears

Which he who loathes shall pity—yea, with tears.

*[*OEDIPUS *is led in, blinded and bleeding. The Old Men bow down and hide their faces; some of them weep.*

CHORUS.

Oh, terrible! Oh, sight of all

This life hath crossed, most terrible!
Thou man more wronged than tongue can tell,
What madness took thee? Do there crawl
Live Things of Evil from the deep
To leap on man? Oh, what a leap
Was His that flung thee to thy fall!

LEADER.

O fallen, fallen in ghastly case,
I dare not raise mine eyes to thee;
Fain would I look and ask and see,
But shudder sickened from thy face.

OEDIPUS.

Oh, pain; pain and woe!
Whither? Whither?
They lead me and I go;
And my voice drifts on the air
Far away.
Where, Thing of Evil, where
Endeth thy leaping hither?

LEADER.

In fearful ends, which none may hear nor say.

Oedipus.

Cloud of the dark, mine own[Strophe.
For ever, horrible,
Stealing, stealing, silent, unconquerable,
Cloud that no wind, no summer can dispel!
Again, again I groan,
As through my heart together crawl the strong
Stabs of this pain and memories of old wrong.

Leader.

Yea, twofold hosts of torment hast thou there,
The stain to think on and the pain to bear.

Oedipus.

O Friend, thou mine own[Antistrophe.
Still faithful, minister
Steadfast abiding alone of them that were,
Dost bear with me and give the blind man care?
Ah me! Not all unknown
Nor hid thou art. Deep in this dark a call
Comes and I know thy voice in spite of all.

Leader.

O fearful sufferer, and could'st thou kill
Thy living orbs? What God made blind thy will?

OEDIPUS.

'Tis Apollo; all is Apollo,[Strophe.

O ye that love me, 'tis he long time hath planned

These things upon me evilly, evilly,

Dark things and full of blood.

I knew not; I did but follow

His way; but mine the hand

And mine the anguish. What were mine eyes to me

When naught to be seen was good?

LEADER.

'Tis even so; and Truth doth speak in thee.

OEDIPUS.

To see, to endure, to hear words kindly spoken,

Should I have joy in such?

Out, if ye love your breath,

Cast me swift unto solitude, unbroken

By word or touch.

Am I not charged with death,

Most charged and filled to the brim

With curses? And what man saith

God hath so hated him?

LEADER.

Thy bitter will, thy hard calamity,

Would I had never known nor looked on thee!

Oedipus.

My curse, my curse upon him,[Antistrophe.

That man whom pity held in the wilderness,

Who saved the feet alive from the blood-fetter

And loosed the barb thereof!

That babe—what grace was done him,

Had he died shelterless,

He had not laid on himself this grief to bear,

And all who gave him love.

Leader.

I, too, O Friend, I had been happier.

Oedipus.

Found not the way to his father's blood, nor shaken

The world's scorn on his mother,

The child and the groom withal;

But now, of murderers born, of God forsaken,

Mine own sons' brother;

All this, and if aught can fall

Upon man more perilous

And elder in sin, lo, all

Is the portion of Oedipus.

LEADER.

How shall I hold this counsel of thy mind
True? Thou wert better dead than living blind.

OEDIPUS.

That this deed is not well and wisely wrought
Thou shalt not show me; therefore school me not.
Think, with what eyes hereafter in the place
Of shadows could I see my father's face,
Or my poor mother's? Both of whom this hand
Hath wronged too deep for man to understand.
Or children—born as mine were born, to see
Their shapes should bring me joy? Great God!
To me
There is no joy in city nor in tower
Nor temple, from all whom, in this mine hour,
I that was chief in Thebes alone, and ate
The King's bread, I have made me separate
For ever. Mine own lips have bid the land
Cast from it one so evil, one whose hand
To sin was dedicate, whom God hath shown
Birth-branded ... and my blood the dead King's own!
All this myself have proved. And can I then
Look with straight eyes into the eyes of men?

I trow not. Nay, if any stop there were
To dam this fount that welleth in mine ear
For hearing, I had never blenched nor stayed
Till this vile shell were all one dungeon made,
Dark, without sound. 'Tis thus the mind would fain
Find peace, self-prisoned from a world of pain.
O wild Kithairon, why was it thy will
To save me? Why not take me quick and kill,
Kill, before ever I could make men know
The thing I am, the thing from which I grow?
Thou dead King, Polybus, thou city wall
Of Corinth, thou old castle I did call
My father's, what a life did ye begin,
What splendour rotted by the worm within,
When ye bred me! O Crossing of the Roads,
O secret glen and dusk of crowding woods,
O narrow footpath creeping to the brink
Where meet the Three! I gave you blood to drink.
Do ye remember? 'Twas my life-blood, hot
From mine own father's heart. Have ye forgot
What deed I did among you, and what new
And direr deed I fled from you to do?
O flesh, horror of flesh!...

But what is shame

To do should not be spoken. In God's name,

Take me somewhere far off and cover me

From sight, or slay, or cast me to the sea

Where never eye may see me any more.

What? Do ye fear to touch a man so sore

Stricken? Nay, tremble not. My misery

Is mine, and shall be borne by none but me.

LEADER.

Lo, yonder comes for answer to thy prayer

Creon, to do and to decree. The care

Of all our land is his, now thou art weak.

OEDIPUS.

Alas, what word to Creon can I speak,

How make him trust me more? He hath seen of late

So vile a heart in me, so full of hate.

Enter CREON.

CREON.

Not to make laughter, Oedipus, nor cast

Against thee any evil of the past

I seek thee, but ... Ah God! ye ministers,

Have ye no hearts? Or if for man there stirs

No pity in you, fear at least to call

Stain on our Lord the Sun, who feedeth all;

Nor show in nakedness a horror such
As this, which never mother Earth may touch,
Nor God's clean rain nor sunlight. Quick within!
Guide him.—The ills that in a house have been
They of the house alone should know or hear.

OEDIPUS.

In God's name, since thou hast undone the fear
Within me, coming thus, all nobleness,
To one so vile, grant me one only grace.
For thy sake more I crave it than mine own.

CREON.

Let me first hear what grace thou wouldst be shown.

OEDIPUS.

Cast me from Thebes ... now, quick ... where none may see
My visage more, nor mingle words with me.

CREON.

That had I done, for sure, save that I still
Tremble, and fain would ask Apollo's will.

OEDIPUS.

His will was clear enough, to stamp the unclean
Thing out, the bloody hand, the heart of sin.

CREON.

'Twas thus he seemed to speak; but in this sore
Strait we must needs learn surer than before.

OEDIPUS.

Thou needs must trouble God for one so low?

CREON.

Surely; thyself will trust his answer now.

OEDIPUS.

I charge thee more ... and, if thou fail, my sin
Shall cleave to thee.... For her who lies within,
Make as thou wilt her burial. 'Tis thy task
To tend thine own. But me: let no man ask
This ancient city of my sires to give
Harbour in life to me. Set me to live
On the wild hills and leave my name to those
Deeps of Kithairon which my father chose,
And mother, for my vast and living tomb.
As they, my murderers, willed it, let my doom
Find me. For this my very heart doth know,
No sickness now, nor any mortal blow,
Shall slay this body. Never had my breath
Been thus kept burning in the midst of death,
Save for some frightful end. So, let my way

Go where it listeth.

But my children—Nay,

Creon, my sons will ask thee for no care.

Men are they, and can find them everywhere

What life needs. But my two poor desolate

Maidens.... There was no table ever set

Apart for them, but whatso royal fare

I tasted, they were with me and had share

In all.... Creon, I pray, forget them not.

And if it may be, go, bid them be brought,

[**CREON** *goes and presently returns with the two princesses.* **OEDIPUS** *thinks he is there all the time.*

That I may touch their faces, and so weep....

Go, Prince. Go, noble heart!...

If I might touch them, I should seem to keep

And not to have lost them, now mine eyes are gone....

What say I?

In God's name, can it be I hear mine own

Beloved ones sobbing? Creon of his grace

Hath brought my two, my dearest, to this place.

Is it true?

CREON.

'Tis true. I brought them, for in them I know

Thy joy is, the same now as long ago.

Oedipus.

God bless thee, and in this hard journey give
Some better guide than mine to help thee live.
Children! Where are ye? Hither; come to these
Arms of your ... brother, whose wild offices
Have brought much darkness on the once bright eyes
Of him who grew your garden; who, nowise
Seeing nor understanding, digged a ground
The world shall shudder at. Children, my wound
Is yours too, and I cannot meet your gaze
Now, as I think me what remaining days
Of bitter living the world hath for you.
What dance of damsels shall ye gather to,
What feast of Thebes, but quick ye shall turn home,
All tears, or ere the feast or dancers come?
And, children, when ye reach the years of love,
Who shall dare wed you, whose heart rise above
The peril, to take on him all the shame
That cleaves to my name and my children's name?
God knows, it is enough!...
My flowers, ye needs must die, waste things, bereft
And fruitless.

Creon, thou alone art left
Their father now, since both of us are gone
Who cared for them. Oh, leave them not alone
To wander masterless, these thine own kin,
And beggared. Neither think of them such sin
As ye all know in me, but let their fate
Touch thee. So young they are, so desolate—
Of all save thee. True man, give me thine hand,
And promise.

*[*OEDIPUS *and* CREON *clasp hands.*

If your age could understand,
Children, full many counsels I could give.
But now I leave this one word: Pray to live
As life may suffer you, and find a road
To travel easier than your father trod.

CREON.

Enough thy heart hath poured its tears; now back into thine house repair.

OEDIPUS.

I dread the house, yet go I must.

CREON.

Fair season maketh all things fair.

OEDIPUS.

One oath then give me, and I go.

CREON.

Name it, and I will answer thee.

OEDIPUS.

To cast me from this land.

CREON.

A gift not mine but God's thou askest me.

OEDIPUS.

I am a thing of God abhorred.

CREON.

The more, then, will he grant thy prayer.

OEDIPUS.

Thou givest thine oath?

CREON.

I see no light; and, seeing not, I may not swear.

OEDIPUS.

Then take me hence. I care not.

CREON.

Go in peace, and give these children o'er.

OEDIPUS.

Ah no! Take not away my daughters!

[They are taken from him.

CREON.

Seek not to be master more.

Did not thy masteries of old forsake thee when the end was near?

CHORUS.

Ye citizens of Thebes, behold; 'tis Oedipus that passeth here,

Who read the riddle-word of Death, and mightiest stood of mortal men,

And Fortune loved him, and the folk that saw him turned and looked again.

Lo, he is fallen, and around great storms and the outreaching sea!

Therefore, O Man, beware, and look toward the end of things that be,

The last of sights, the last of days; and no man's life account as gain

Ere the full tale be finished and the darkness find him without pain.

*[*OEDIPUS *is led into the house and the doors close on him.*

9 789358 481495

Printed at Repro India Ltd.